CW00735511

FIND YOUR POWER

MEDITATION

An Hachette UK Company
www.hachette.co.uk

First published in Great Britain in 2023 by Godsfield,
an imprint of Octopus Publishing Group Ltd
Carmelite House, 50 Victoria Embankment, London EC4Y 0DZ
www.octopusbooks.co.uk

Copyright © Octopus Publishing Group Ltd 2023

All rights reserved. No part of this work may be reproduced or utilized in any form
or by any means, electronic or mechanical, including photocopying, recording or by
any information storage and retrieval system, without the prior written permission of
the publisher.

ISBN 978-1-8418-1553-4

A CIP catalogue record for this book is available from the British Library

Printed and bound in China

10 9 8 7 6 5 4 3 2 1

Publisher: Lucy Pessell
Designer: Isobel Platt
Editor: Feyi Oyesanya
Assistant Editor: Samina Rahman
Production Controller: Allison Gonsalves

This FSC® label means that materials used for the product have been responsibly sourced

FIND YOUR POWER

MEDITATION

EMILY HERSEY

GODSFIELD

CONTENTS

FIND YOUR POWER

When daily life becomes busy and your time and energy is pulled in many different directions, it can be difficult to find time to nourish yourself. Prioritizing your own wellbeing can be a struggle and you risk feeling overwhelmed, unsure of where to turn and what you need in order to feel lighter and find your inner strength.

Taking some time to focus on yourself, answering questions you may be avoiding or facing problems that are simmering away under the surface is the best gift you can give yourself. But it can be difficult to know where to start.

Sometimes all you need to learn life's big lessons is a little guidance. In this series of books you will learn about personal healing, self-empowerment and how to nourish your spirit. Explore practices which will help you to get clear on what you really want, and that will encourage you to acknowledge – and deal with – any limiting beliefs or negative thoughts that might be holding you back in living life to your fullest power.

These books provide invaluable advice on how to create the best conditions for a healthier, happier, and more fulfilled life. Bursting with essential background, revealing insights and useful activities and exercises to enable you to understand and expand your personal practices every day, it's time to delve into your spiritual journey and truly Find Your Power.

Other titles in the series:
- *Find Your Power: Tarot*
- *Find Your Power: Manifest*
- *Find Your Power: Numerology*
- *Find Your Power: Runes*
- *Find Your Power: Crystals*
- *Find Your Power: Mindfulness*
- *Find Your Power: Chakras*

INTRODUCTION

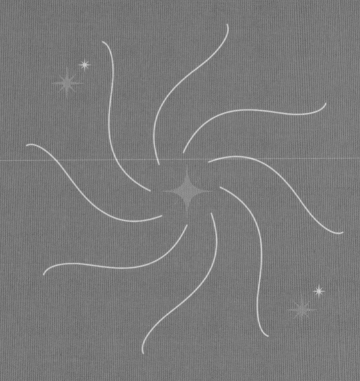

People come to meditation for various reasons and with different expectations. Initially, it is enough to approach your meditation practice as just another element of your daily exercise routine and take from it whatever you need, be it relief from stress, improved physical and mental health or a sustained sense of wellbeing. In time, as your awareness increases, you may feel the urge to explore altered states of consciousness in search of the answers to the questions that fascinate us all. If, and when, you are ready to do so, you will find a number of exercises in the final sections of this book that will guide you safely to discover what is true for you.

Meditation's considerable biological benefits include regulating blood pressure, stimulating blood circulation, alleviating pain and reducing muscular tension. It can even slow down hormonal activity, so that people who practise meditation on a regular basis begin to look healthier and feel fitter.

Even if you feel physically fit and healthy there are considerable benefits to be gained from integrating meditation into your daily routine. By practising it regularly you can develop self-discipline, improve your personal performance in sports, business and the arts, build self-confidence, increase your energy and efficiency, and generally create a more positive attitude to life.

But in addition to the proven psycho-biological benefits meditation can be the first step on the path to self-discovery and greater awareness leading ultimately to Enlightenment, where we attain a state of detachment which the Buddhists describe as being 'in the world but not of it'.

WHY MEDITATE?

As Lao Tzu, the great Chinese philosopher and founder of Taoism, remarked, 'the thousand-mile journey begins with one step', and on the long journey towards self-awareness meditation provides that first significant step. It provides us with a quiet time for ourselves, time to discover who we really are and what we want from life. Practised twice daily (morning and evening) for as little as ten minutes at a time it offers the opportunity for each of us to create what is effectively a sacred space in which to nurture a sense of wellbeing, tap our inner resources and find lasting peace of mind.

It is a common myth that meditation is only for people who are 'spiritually advanced'. Anyone can meditate if they put their mind to it. As with any activity that requires a degree of self-discipline it becomes easier with practice and pleasantly addictive, once you begin to feel the benefits.

We all meditate in one form or another whenever we lose ourselves in a routine task, in music or a film, for example, or when we are transfixed by the beauty of nature. However, such moments are rare and fleeting. Through passive contemplation or active concentration, meditation can harness this capacity for detachment at will so that we can learn to still our scattered thoughts and focus our mind.

In this heightened state of awareness, the body is relaxed and we are no longer self-centred but centred within our 'true nature'. Having attained this blissful state, there is then the opportunity to use meditation for examining the psyche. This includes exploring the unconscious and experiencing the inner and external dimensions of the spirit from which we can derive insights, guidance and a profound understanding of the nature of existence and the part that we have chosen to play in its unfolding.

It is a common misconception that meditation and conventional forms of relaxation are the same thing. However, meditation is not the passive act that it appears, and when practised regularly it has the potential to bring far greater benefits than simple relaxation.

While relaxation offers temporary relief from stress, meditation aims to achieve both relaxation of the body and a heightened state of awareness. Regular meditation can help to bring greater control over your restless thoughts and emotions leading to a sense of wellbeing.

The practice of meditation has a cumulative effect, and the benefits can be felt almost immediately – a sense of detachment from the pressures of life and lasting peace of mind.

INNER DEPTHS

According to Eastern philosophy and the Western esoteric tradition, the source of wisdom and inspiration is within. Whether we call this wisdom the 'Higher Self', the Soul, our Buddha nature or the Christ Consciousness, it is both the immortal essence of our being and an indivisible element of the 'Universal Mind'.

One of the aims of meditation is to subdue the restless chattering of the ego (the conscious mind) and train it to submit to the 'Higher Self' so that we can achieve an expansion of consciousness at will. When we attain this altered state, we experience supreme understanding and the bliss of true peace which is known as Enlightenment.

Contrary to popular belief Enlightenment is not limited to ascetics, saints or mystics. It is within the grasp of everyone to manifest their 'true nature' within their lifetime, for we are, in essence, Divine.

Meditation offers us the means by which we can heighten our sensitivity to the still, small voice within ourselves and transcend our physical perception to glimpse the 'Greater Reality' that is beyond. Various traditions have developed different techniques for achieving this.

The practice of meditation has a cumulative effect, and the benefits can be felt almost immediately.

By adopting a balanced
and relaxed posture we can
attain a state of serenity
and heightened awareness.

THE BUDDHIST RELIGION

Buddhism makes no distinction between sacred and secular life; every act is performed as if it is the subject of meditation. In Buddhism, as in many other traditions, meditation is not seen as something that is to be mastered, but as a state of mind that we can slip into in the same way that we relax when our daily work is done.

Once we find peace of mind, we are not to try to possess it, but rather to remain in a state of 'calm abiding'. When thoughts arise, they should be considered as transient and insignificant as ripples on the surface of a lake that will return to tranquillity. In this serene state negativity, aggression and confusion simply cannot exist.

ZEN BUDDHISM

In the form of Zen Buddhism known as Rinzai, teachers lead their pupils towards enlightenment by confounding their rational minds with an enigmatic form of riddle known as a *koan* so that the inner chatter is silenced and intuition takes over. A typical exchange was that which took place between the Indian sage Bodhidharma and a pupil who pleaded with his master to pacify his mind to which the Bodhidharma replied, 'Show me your mind.' When the pupil confessed that it was impossible, his master remarked, 'There, I have pacified your mind.'

Koans are a technique particular to Rinzai, which roughly translates as 'sudden'. It describes a direct, confrontational form which is intended to shock the mind into a state in which perceptions and values are rendered meaningless so that the initiate can accept a new reality. In contrast, Soto Zen requires its followers to practise a 'Serene Reflection' method that involves sitting in silence and allowing the mind to settle like silt gently stirred up in a muddy pond. Once this state has been attained, acute awareness, and ultimately Enlightenment, follow naturally. Zen tends to confound the logical mind because it contradicts the belief that life has a meaning. Instead Zen philosophy says that life is simply a moment of being.

HINDU BELIEFS

In the Hindu tradition there are ten distinct limbs of yoga, all leading to Enlightenment. *Dhyana* yoga is the form concerned with meditation, while *Laya* yoga seeks to manifest the divine spark by stimulating the chakras, the subtle energy centres situated in the etheric, or spiritual, body. One way in which this can be done is to use meditations where the initiate visualizes these vortices as blossoming lotus flowers of varying colours (see pages 118–121).

Dhyana yoga has two approaches. The first is called *Saguna*, and here the mind is focused on an object, mantra (sacred words for concentration) or symbol, to the extent that all sense of physical reality is rendered meaningless. In the second, *Nirguna*, the subject of the meditation is abstract and in this approach the initiate seeks total absorption. Either approach sees yoga as a form of meditation with each of the yoga asanas, or postures, being a form of meditation in action.

TRANSCENDENTAL MEDITATION

TM was introduced to the West in 1958 by Maharishi Mahesh Yogi and since then it has been adopted by celebrities, elite sports personalties and life coaches.

In 1987 a leading Japanese company, Sumitomo Heavy Industries, introduced TM

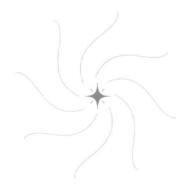

What really matters is not just the practice of sitting but far more the state of mind you find yourself in after meditation. It is this calm and centred state of mind you should prolong through everything you do.

to 600 of its managers and monitored their progress and productivity over the following 18 months. Sumitomo recorded a considerable drop in absenteeism and a significant increase in individual performance and quality of work. The managers claimed their health had improved and that they suffered less from stress which in turn gave them a happier home life.

Although the four million practitioners of TM worldwide make great claims for its psycho-biological benefits, in essence it is no different from any other meditation technique and therefore the claims made for its effectiveness can apply equally to all forms of meditation. It differs from traditional forms of meditation in only one respect; it emphasizes the importance of adopting a personal mantra which is to be kept secret from the other members of the group. This is one reason why TM has been criticized for cultivating a cult-like clique. The other is that it prohibits anyone other than a teacher who has been personally trained by its founder, Maharishi Mahesh Yogi, from teaching the technique.

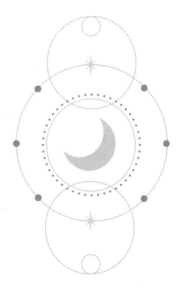

STARTING TO MEDITATE

It's a common myth that meditation comes more easily to individuals of Eastern extraction. Meditation is the natural state of the mind, but Western culture has made it difficult for Americans and Europeans, in particular, to establish the habit. From early childhood we are constantly bombarded with external stimuli until we become addicted to seeking sensation. We are conditioned from birth to seek stimulation and satisfaction of all the senses – whether it be in food, fashion, entertainment, drink or drugs, the ultimate 'quick fix'. We are made to feel self-conscious, anti-social and even eccentric if we express the need to take time out for ourselves to meditate. While many people have embraced yoga in their regular exercise routine, meditation is still often seen as slightly strange and self-indulgent.

For these reasons Westerners have an inner resistance to meditation, on principle. So this is the first major hurdle that you will need to overcome if you want to meditate regularly.

MAKING TIME TO MEDITATE

Initially you will probably find lots of other things that seem in more urgent need of your attention, and you will be tempted to put off your meditation time indefinitely. Do not do that. There is no better time to start meditating than the present, so when you have finished reading this sentence: shut the book, close your eyes, and take a few minutes to sit in silence.

As for all those things that you feel you ought to be doing instead of meditating, persevere and you will soon find that you readily put off everything else in order to meditate. It is then that you will have to be careful that you do not become hooked on the experience.

In certain respects meditation is no different to physical exercise. Both require a certain amount of self-discipline if the habit is to be established. It is a good idea to meditate at the same time every day, even if it is only for ten minutes, so encourage yourself by making that time of the day a special time. Create an inviting atmosphere with candles, incense and a small vase of fresh lightly scented flowers (see pages 26–27).

It will also help if you have a specific focus for each session,

There is no better time to start meditating than the present.

> It is important to sample the various methods of meditation before deciding on the one which suits you.

such as sending your healing force to people you know who are in need, or to a particular area of the world where people are suffering (see pages 60–62). Absent healing is one of the best ways to cultivate compassion and to stop being so self-centred, which are two essential steps on the path to peace of mind and, ultimately, to Enlightenment.

LEARNING TO RELAX

Another thing that you will need to nurture is the ability to relax. We all assume that relaxation comes naturally to us, but it does not. We have been conditioned to believe that we must constantly be active and productive. A certain amount of stress can be stimulating because it releases adrenaline, which is energizing in certain situations, but we can become addicted to that natural chemical 'high'. That is why it is important to establish a balance between mental or physical activity and quiet contemplation.

When we do relax it tends to be in a passive, unfocused way. This is dissimilar from the meditation experience which aims for heightened awareness and total relaxation of the body. I often think of meditation as being similar to swimming, as to be successful at either depends on the ability to relax. If you relax in the water, you will find it easier to swim because the water will support you, but if you become tense you will sink.

It is important to sample the various methods of meditation before deciding on the one which suits you.

Give each one a fair trial, perhaps practising it ten minutes a day for a week, before moving onto the next. I have known plenty of students who came to my classes expecting to respond to quiet contemplation, for example, but who found themselves hooked by the inner visions that arose in them during creative visualization exercises.

GOOD MEDITATION PRACTICE

There are several points to bear in mind before you start meditating on a regular basis.

- Consider keeping a journal of your experiences and insights as the significance of certain details may only become apparent after subsequent sessions.

- It is not a good idea to eat a heavy meal if you are planning to meditate within the next hour as

the physiological functions slow down the digestion.

- If you do feel uneasy for any reason during a meditation simply count down slowly from ten to one and return to waking consciousness. If you do this, you will invariably find that the anxiety goes before you open your eyes and so you can continue the exercise.

- Do not be surprised if you find yourself worrying whether a spider might be crawling around while you have your eyes closed. When these thoughts occur simply bring your attention gently back to the subject of the exercise.

- Unexpected noises can be a distraction during meditation, but only if you let them. The banging of a door, a car horn and so on are gone in a moment, but if you worry about how you might react if it happens again, or despair of getting perfect peace

and quiet, you empower them with life beyond that moment. It is comparatively easy to meditate in perfect silence, the real test is to remain relaxed and focused in the real world.

- Finally, ensure your privacy and peace as much as possible. Take the phone off the hook or put the answering machine on and put a sign on the door telling flatmates or family that you are not to be disturbed while meditating.

CREATING SACRED SPACES

Meditation can be practised wherever and whenever you feel the need to create a quiet moment, although obviously there are times when you need to be alert and attentive, such as when you are driving a car or working with machinery. Otherwise, it can be beneficial to establish brief mindfulness meditations during a lull at work or a break from routine tasks and long periods of study. You can even meditate while walking (see pages 55). However, most of your practice will presumably be done at home, and although it is not necessary to dedicate a special room or corner of your living space for meditation there are many benefits to be derived from having a special place where you can practise.

CHOOSING YOUR SPACE

The first benefit of having a regular place to meditate is that it helps to establish the routine and break the initial resistance which everybody has to sitting still and staying silent for more than a few minutes. Creating a simple altar, if you desire one, and decorating the area in a suitably calming or neutral colour with pictures and objects that are designed to put you 'in the mood' will make a room feel like your private sanctuary and will put

> **Create an aura of peace in meditation so that you can always take it with you out into the world.**

passive pursuits like watching TV into a new perspective.

The second reason for having a dedicated space is that you will find that the room will soon acquire an ambience that is conducive to meditation and relaxation as it will have been 'charged' by your positive mental energy. Each time you enter the room you will intuitively tune in to these subtle vibrations and find that you settle into meditation more easily as a result of this inviting, therapeutic atmosphere.

MAKING YOUR SANCTUARY

Everyone has their own idea of what an ideal sanctuary might look like for them, but here are a few helpful hints.

- Keep the room simple. The primary aims of meditation are heightened concentration and total absorption in a single idea or object, both of which you will find difficult to achieve in a room that is too cluttered.

- Have something from nature within reach, such as a bowl of water, or a small vase of flowers that could act as a focal object in a specific exercise.

- Symbols of the four elements are also useful tools for contemplation. Represent Earth with a crystal, or a plant; Air with incense; Fire with a candle; and Water with a full ceramic bowl of it. If you do not have a crystal the bowl will double as Earth, as it does in many traditions.

- If you are using candles, always make sure that they are secure, and that the holder is placed in a large bowl of water so that there is no risk of fire.

- The room needs to be comfortably warm and well aired, particularly if you are using candles or incense.

- Wind chimes and soothing music or natural sounds can help to create the right atmosphere.

Of course, you do not need to have a dedicated space for meditation and in time, with regular practice, you will create a sanctuary in your mind so that it will have a reality on the inner levels. As for being able to generate sacred space, you already do this with the influence of the aura that you radiate and that is why it is important that you create an aura of peace in meditation so that you can always take it with you out into the world.

GETTING OFF THE GROUND

This chapter describes the principles of posture and breath control before presenting a set of simple meditations to help to establish the habit and the foundations of good practice. These preliminary exercises will help you to develop greater powers of visualization, concentration and deep relaxation as well as an acute awareness of the mind and physical body in action. The distinction between active and passive meditation is also outlined, together with a look at how to bring meditation into daily life through a form of heightened awareness known as 'mindfulness'. The section ends with body scanning and grounding exercises to reduce stress and centre you in preparation for more advanced techniques.

POSTURE

When you first start meditating, it is important to try to establish good habits early on, specifically those concerning correct posture and breath control. However, do not become too preoccupied with details. Aim to ease yourself into meditation so that relaxation and serenity soon come as readily as sleep.

Many of the exercises in this book are concerned with stimulating the free flow of energy around the body and of drawing the 'universal life force' that we can all have access to into the head and through the feet. For that reason those meditations should be performed when sitting down. However, general relaxations and visualizations can be performed lying flat on a bed or mat if you prefer.

Whichever form of yogic meditation one adopts, the aim is to lose one's sense of separateness and become absorbed in the silence.

LYING DOWN

If you choose to lie down, lie on an exercise mat or a carpet and make sure that you support your neck with a firm cushion. Let your arms hang loosely by your side and keep your legs straight. Do not cross your legs or put your hands on your body unless you want to use your hands to direct healing energy to a particular area.

SITTING DOWN

Choose a straight-backed chair to sit in so that you get support and do not cramp your diaphragm. Your feet should be flat on the floor and slightly apart in line with your shoulders. Place your hands on your knees, palms down, although you may prefer to have them facing upwards in a symbolic gesture of openness or to send out energy during absent healing. Some people like to adopt the Buddhist practice of cupping their hands in their laps in front of their navels with the tips of their thumbs touching, but such details are a matter of personal choice. As a general rule do whatever feels right and is comfortable for you.

Do not let your chin sink into your chest because it will restrict your breathing. Your chin should be just slightly inclined towards your chest, while you look straight ahead.

CLASSICAL POSTURES

The traditional cross-legged postures that are used in yoga and Buddhism require a degree of suppleness that does not come easily to Westerners. However, you can train yourself to adopt these positions, which you may feel enhance the meditation experience.

These are classical postures, but an alternative position is to rest on your heels with a cushion supporting the buttocks, as in the Japanese tradition described in alternative postures overleaf.

Full Lotus Position: for the full lotus position, place your right foot on your left thigh and your left foot on your right thigh. Rest your palms on your knees. This ensures circulation of energy around the body.

Half Lotus Position: for the less demanding half lotus position, the right foot rests on the left thigh while the left foot lies under the right thigh, or vice versa. Palms can be turned upwards in a receptive gesture or cupped around the knees.

Quarter Lotus Position: this is particularly suitable when you wish to emphasize your openness, i.e. for guidance, self-healing and cleaning meditations. Even less demanding, the right foot rests on the left calf while the left foot lies on the right calf. Rest your palms on your knees.

ALTERNATIVE POSTURES AND HAND POSITIONS

Although the various postures described on these pages are interchangeable, you should attempt all of them initially, persevering with each for a week until settling with one or two that you find particularly suitable. The purpose of the various postures is to discipline the body in the belief that the mind will follow. As you focus your attention on the physical demands of the increasingly difficult positions, the mind will cease its restless chatter, and you will become mindful of the body and so centred more effectively than if you simply sit in a chair and relax.

Both posture and breathing are useful for aiding concentration when your thoughts wander, as they will do in the early stages of meditation. This centring of mind and body will also influence your performance during your daily activities. You will become more confident and efficient because your mind and body are being integrated at the deepest level. Being poised in this way will also help to create a sense of space within yourself where the real work will take place.

These preliminary exercises will help you to develop greater powers of visualization, concentration and deep relaxation.

It is important to
discipline yourself into
maintaining an everyday
period of relaxation
and focusing.

THE IDEAL IMAGE

Choose one of the positions from those described in this chapter and then sit or lie down as preferred, close your eyes, relax and visualize yourself sitting before a large mirror in which is reflected the image of a faceless figure in the position you have chosen. He or she is surrounded by coloured candles and wisps of scented incense smoke. Now look into the world beyond the mirror where the figure lives. It is a serene scene with lush, green valleys and snow-capped mountains in the far distance. Feel yourself being drawn out of your body to merge with this figure. Feel the poise, the serenity that comes from being centred, and the expanding awareness as your mental energy transcends the limitations of your physical body. When you feel ready, gradually return to consciousness.

THE BREATH OF LIFE

Without a doubt the most difficult aspect of meditation to master is the quietening of the mind. Even when we are physically relaxed our minds are still buzzing. Until we can control this restless activity and learn to focus our mental energy it will be diffused, and we will have passed the time reserved for meditation, rather than having used it.

The simplest method of stilling the mind is to focus on a single object or action, for it is impossible to concentrate on two things at the same time. We focus naturally when something interests us, but usually the object of interest is not suitable for meditation. In theory, of course, everything is a suitable subject for meditation, but it is best to keep it simple. That is one reason why the first step is to learn basic breath control.

BASIC BREATH CONTROL

Aim for a regular rhythm which you can help to establish by counting at your own tempo.

1. Close your eyes and let yourself become aware of your breathing.

2. Place your hands in front of your navel and feel your diaphragm move out as you inhale.

3. Move your hands to your chest and feel your lungs expand.

4. With outstretched arms exhale gradually and inhale deeply without forcing the air in or out.

5. Now take as deep a breath as you can comfortably manage, hold it for a count of 4, then let it out like a sigh as slowly as you can until every last particle of bad air has been expelled from your lungs.

6. Now begin to establish a regular rhythm using either a count of 4-2-4-2 or 8-4-8-4. That is, inhaling for a count of 4, holding that breath for a count of 2 before exhaling for a count of 4, then pausing for a count of 2 before taking the next breath.

7. If you find counting to be too mechanical, you can exchange it for a mantra (see pages 95-98) or a simple spoken phrase such as 'peace and calm'. After a few months it should be easy to maintain the rhythm without counting.

8. When you eventually meditate without counting or using a mantra you will find that thoughts arise in the silence. It is then that you will have to cultivate the discipline of detachment by allowing thoughts to arise, observing them without becoming distracted and then returning to the object that you have chosen to focus upon.

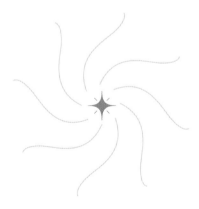

ADVANCED BREATHING TECHNIQUE

Alternate nostril breathing is central to yogic meditation and is proven to be effective in dealing with stress. The techniques given here are adapted from classical yoga and are best performed in the lotus position or cross-legged:

1. Keeping the three main fingers of your right hand closed, extend your thumb and little finger. With the right nostril blocked by your thumb, breathing deeply inhale for five seconds and exhale for five through the left nostril.

2. Bring your third or fourth finger across to block your left nostril, release your thumb.

3. Inhale for five seconds and exhale for five seconds through the right nostril. Repeat the exercise 10 times on the right nostril and 10 times on the left. Next, try inhaling for five seconds, holding for three seconds and exhaling for five seconds. Repeat 10 times on each nostril.

Another variation is as follows:

1. Close your eyes and put your thumb against your right nostril. Place your index and middle fingers over your 'third eye', (situated in the middle of your forehead) while your fourth finger rests against your left nostril.

2. Breathe deeply, exhale then close your right nostril with your thumb. Now gently and deeply inhale through your left nostril for eight seconds. Hold that breath for four seconds and close your left nostril with the fourth finger. Keeping your left nostril closed, release the thumb and slowly exhale for eight seconds through the right nostril.

3. Inhale again through the right nostril for eight seconds. Hold the breath for four seconds and close both nostrils briefly. Open your left nostril and exhale for eight seconds. Begin the cycle again by inhaling through your left nostril.

4. Try to establish a smooth and regular rhythm. Repeat five times, then rest your hand on your knee and sit in silence for a few minutes.

ACTIVE AND PASSIVE MEDITATION

Practitioners of traditional yoga make a distinction between what they call active and passive meditation. Active is defined as the type that is practised while you go about your daily life approaching every experience as a meditation and observing your mind and body in action, while passive requires that you sit still, enter deep relaxation and concentrate.

We tend to think of meditation only in terms of the latter with its emphasis on solitude, stillness and silence, but active meditation is of equal importance in assimilating the benefits of meditation into everyday life.

OBSERVING THE BODY IN ACTION

We all have nervous habits of one kind or another, even if it only amounts to fidgeting while waiting for a bus, but such compulsions to keep active have a debilitating effect on our reserves of vital energy. Instead we should be conserving this energy, while remaining mentally alert. Relaxation is not just for those moments when we are doing nothing but should be incorporated into our physical activities so that we can be productive with the minimum of effort.

You will also find that you have more energy if you minimize the small talk that is believed to fritter away the life force. As has often

been said, many of us talk a lot but say very little worth hearing. We tend to make small talk to fill the silence, but it is only in the silence that inspiration and insights can be heard.

OBSERVING THE ORDINARY MIND

Whether your daily routine tends to be repetitive and mundane or stimulating and stressful, you will learn much about yourself by becoming an observer of what is known as the ordinary, conscious mind, the 'I' with which we readily identify, or what orthodox psychology terms the ego. Note when your conscious mind is concentrated on a task, or wandering, because when it is unfocused you are wasting vital mental energy.

Do you indulge in aimless wish-fulfilment, or in self-criticism over past mistakes? Do you fantasize about the future then fail to take the necessary steps to nurture these seeds to fruition?

Such problems stem from a lack of focus in life and a lack of control over the thought processes. We may all possess brains with the capacity of a supercomputer, but in practice our thoughts tend to get stuck in a groove like a stylus in an old vinyl record, playing the same old song until even the most negative thoughts have a familiar and comfortable ring about them. Becoming aware of the way in which the conscious mind undermines our efforts is the first step towards training the mind so that we can free ourselves from such bad habits and tap into our subconscious and hidden potential.

When you become aware of negative thoughts do not let them run amok in your mind. Corner them and affirm that you disown such debilitating ideas.

While we know the value of physical relaxation, we tend to keep the mind switched on in the same way that some people keep the radio running from breakfast to bedtime in the hope that something interesting will eventually come on. But just as tension in the body can leave us tired and strained, the mind too, when burdened with anxieties and in need of rest, can cease to function efficiently. So make time for mental as well as physical relaxation or you risk potential overload. It is said that 'those who have no time for meditation will have plenty of time for sickness and suffering.'

MINDFULNESS

Mindfulness is one of the simplest forms of meditation and potentially the most revealing as it involves letting go of any desire to control your thoughts. Instead, you should try to observe them with detachment as they arise spontaneously, together with any emotions, physical sensations, sounds and images that compete for your attention. You attach no importance to them because if you allow yourself to be distracted, they will assume a significance that they do not deserve. In effect, you accept no responsibility for your thoughts, but consider them to be insignificant because they have no intrinsic reality.

To find lasting peace of mind we first have to accept that we cannot control our thoughts, only our response to them, and in doing so we make peace with our minds. Eventually, you should come to an understanding of the nature of the mind through such meditations and find freedom from its content, for the mind deceives by creating the illusion that we can return to the past or anticipate the future using memory and imagination. But, in fact, we exist only in the present. That is the nature of consciousness and the one reality that we can experience in mindfulness meditation.

Some people who have difficulty with more 'conventional' forms of meditation which demand that we master our mental processes find mindfulness easier because it acknowledges that we cannot control our thoughts. Instead we watch them flit across our mental screen like birds in flight while we remain focused on a fixed point on the horizon.

USING MINDFULNESS

You can practise mindfulness in the traditional sitting posture if you prefer, but you should try to practise it when doing things that require your full attention such as eating. Eating is a particularly good example of something that should be performed in the state of mindfulness because only in that state will we really enjoy our food and derive the most nourishment possible from it.

Ultimately, every act from performing routine chores to making love should be performed in this relaxed state of awareness.

As a modern master of meditiation wrote, 'Everything can be used as an invitation to meditation.'

✳

To find lasting peace of mind we first have to accept that we cannot control our thoughts.

✳

SIMPLE MEDITATIONS

In meditation, as in other mental and physical disciplines, it is important to begin with simple exercises to establish good practice. These basic meditations will help you to establish the habit of sitting still in silence and will train your mind to focus on the object of the exercise. If you attempt the more demanding disciplines, such as guided visualizations, before you are comfortable with the basic techniques, then you may find that your mind wanders. You may also find that the quality of relaxation and awareness is diminished or unsatisfactory and that consequently, you will not be able to trust the guidance and insights that may come through.

Choose one of these exercises and practise it once or better still twice a day for six days, then rest for one day before moving on to the next exercise. After you become comfortable with them all and you can retain the images in your mind for at least five minutes, move on to experiment with other techniques, but use these freely whenever you need to test your powers of concentration, or you need a few minutes of quiet for yourself during the day.

If you wish, they can also become part of your regular routine as supplements to the main meditations as they will prepare the mind for deeper relaxation and explorations into the subconscious.

DOT MEDITATION

Get into your chosen position (see pages 31–33). Close your eyes, breathe naturally (see pages 36–38) and when you feel suitably relaxed, begin to visualize a tiny white dot directly in front of you against the darkness.

1. When you have had the dot fixed in your mind for several minutes without distraction, then visualize it growing larger and larger until you can step into it.

2. At this point open your eyes and sit still for a few moments before returning to whatever task you had been performing previously.

3. Try substituting the dot with a number the next time you attempt this exercise, and when you have mastered that try to visualize a coloured circle or light. It is not as easy as you think and you may find these exercises boring, but it is vital that you develop these basic skills before you move on.

CANDLE MEDITATION

Sit in your chosen position and breathe naturally.

1. Focus on a lighted candle and soften your gaze so that you are looking slightly beyond the flame. When you feel that you have retained it in your mind's eye, close your eyes and keep the flame as steady as you can. At first the afterglow will fade, and you will be left with nothing, so you will need to open your eyes again and repeat the process.

2. Eventually you will have a mental image of the candle that is distinct from the afterglow, and you should be able to retain this for some minutes. When you achieve this level of concentration let go and lose yourself in the flame. Become one with the flame so that there is no space between it and you. Enjoy the sense of spaciousness and expansion.

3. When you feel ready, slowly come back to waking consciousness and open your eyes.

FOCUSING ON INANIMATE OBJECTS

Inanimate objects are commonly used as a focus for meditation in both the Eastern and Western traditions. You will need to incorporate a 'still-life' meditation in your own routine from time to time as it helps to develop the ability to meditate with your eyes open which, in time, will evolve into the discipline of heightened awareness known as mindfulness (see pages 44–45).

USING SIMPLE OBJECTS

Initially, choose a simple object that has as few features as possible, such as an apple, a paperweight or a plain vase. If you decide to focus on a plant, choose a simple form with leaves of one colour. You can increase the complexity of the objects in due course as your ability develops, but do not choose something that

has any significance for you as you do not want to be distracted by memories or images associated with the object.

Place the object just beyond arm's length so that it is situated between eye-level and that of the navel when you are seated so that you do not put any strain on your neck when looking down it for any length of time. Ensure that you place it on a plain surface that is clear of all other items, otherwise you might be distracted and unable to concentrate on the chosen object.

FOCUSING ON AN OBJECT

Get into your chosen position. Close your eyes, take a deep breath, hold it for a few moments, then exhale slowly. When you feel sufficiently relaxed, open your eyes and soften your gaze as you focus on the object. Do not try to memorize its features, but just observe it as if it's a bud about to blossom, or a musical box that will play an enchanting melody.

1. Allow the background to fade into soft focus as you zoom in on the object. Become aware of its texture, colour and form. Take your time as you do this. Do not let yourself become impatient to move on to the next part of the exercise.

2. Visualize yourself touching it, tasting it and smelling it; again, take your time. This is not a chore that needs to be done, it is the doing that is the whole purpose of the exercise.

3. This is a good point at which to end the meditation when you are a beginner (go to the countdown at the end), but when you feel ready to go further than this you can add the following stages.

4. Imagine that you have been shrunk to the size of an ant and can explore the object. Look back from that perspective and see yourself sitting in the chair. If this is difficult at first, persevere, as this ability to develop a sense of detachment and focus your awareness elsewhere is important.

5. Imagine the processes that were involved in the manufacture or growth of this object and then the stages involved in bringing it to you. Visualize its part in the hierarchy of nature, the forces that brought it into being and the purpose of its existence. Even a paperweight or a pebble has a purpose and an indispensable place in existence, for everything in existence is interconnected. As you become aware of this, the boundary between the objective and subjective will become blurred and you will become part of what you perceive. As your awareness increases, the object will become suffused with meaning.

6. When you are completely ready, return to waking consciousness by counting down from ten to one and stamping your feet to reaffirm your return to the physical world.

WARM-UP

Although a physical warm-up routine may appear unnecessary to your meditation practice, it is useful in freeing energy blockages that tend to occur in the head, neck and back. We usually remain unaware of these blockages until we focus on this area. Warming up loosens the muscles and gives a sensation of expansion and openness. Relaxation and breath control will be more difficult to achieve if the body is cramped and allowed to slump or slouch. The neck, head and shoulders tend to lock up with tension and stress. A few simple warm-up exercises will help to loosen these muscles and will open the upper body in readiness for deep relaxation.

- Move your head forwards and backwards before finishing with a few side-to-side movements tilting your right ear to your right shoulder, then repeat with the left.

- Raise both shoulders as high as you can, tense the muscles, hold for a few moments and relax. Then roll the shoulders a few times, first forwards and then backwards.

- Wrinkling your forehead will help to dissipate tension and stress.

- Clenching your teeth and pulling a face heightens awareness of stress and can lighten you up.

HOW TO CENTRE YOURSELF

This is a type of 'warming-up' exercise for deeper meditations and involves further visualization techniques. It can be used at a time of extreme emotional stress when you feel the need to bring yourself back down to earth, to 'centre' or ground yourself. Perform this exercise while sitting in a chair with your back straight and your feet flat on the floor.

GROUNDING

Begin by focusing on your breathing. As you exhale, visualize the tension that has been trapped being released inside your body in the form of smoke. Visualize it as a form of energy pollution that you have involuntarily absorbed as you might do with exhaust fumes.

1. You have no need of tension. It serves no useful function. See it seeping from your toes, the hips, and solar plexus (middle of your stomach).

2. See it gathering in your stomach, rising through your chest, and out through your nostrils with every exhalation. Free yourself from this tension by visualizing it dispersing like smoke with each out breath that you make.

3. Now that your body's clear once again, you need to revitalize yourself with an infusion of the 'Universal Force'. Begin by visualizing a point just above your head and see a sphere of incandescent light appear like the sun in the noon sky. As you focus on this light with your inner eye it intensifies in brilliance. It descends upon you, and you begin to inhale the light as you would fresh air or an intoxicating incense.

4. Absorb the energy as you breathe. Feel the warmth saturating through your arms to your hands and fingertips. It courses down through the rest of your body. You feel refreshed, invigorated and renewed. Now there is nothing but the light circulating throughout your system.

5. Now visualize a second sphere of almost translucent light, like the full moon in the clear night sky emerging from the earth. Begin to draw this light up through the soles of your feet and into your body. Sense the different quality of this energy rising up through your body.

6. Feel the two streams of celestial and terrestrial energy blending in your physical body and permeating the other levels of your being. You are now fully energized and grounded.

7. Bathe in the light for as long as you wish, before slowly returning to waking consciousness by counting down slowly from ten to one. As you count down, focus once again on your breathing and become aware of your body, the chair you are sitting on and your surroundings. When you feel ready, open your eyes.

MEDITATION
IN MOTION

In the West we tend to equate meditation with sitting in silence, but there is a long tradition of walking meditations among spiritual seekers of all persuasions, from the religious pilgrim who travels vast distances to visit a shrine to the Myanma Buddhist monk who can take all day to cross a courtyard. Walking meditations as a formal discipline are thought to have developed after Buddha urged his followers to leave their homes in search of Enlightenment, and they continue to offer a counterbalance to the introspective practice of sitting in silence.

HOLISTIC HEALING

This section explores how you can stimulate the subtle energy centres known in the Hindu tradition as the 'chakras' for the purposes of self-, absent and planetary healing.

It also describes how you can channel this vital Universal Force to protect yourself from negative influences and revitalize yourself whenever you are stressed or depleted of energy. It concludes with a description of how the four elements correspond to aspects of the human psyche and outlines how you can work with these natural forces to increase your self-awareness and psychic sensitivity, or intuition.

SELF-HEALING AND HEALING OTHERS

It is now generally accepted that the cause of many physical disorders is a deeply rooted dis-ease in the mind or psyche, and not simply a random biological breakdown in the body. If this is so, then it should be possible to restore balance to the whole of our being by removing the blockage or blockages which we have created in order to draw attention to our unhappiness.

The first step towards self-healing is to admit that we may have unconsciously manifested symptoms because we fear the strength of our own emotions. If, for example, we lose a loved one and deny ourselves the cleansing process that is grief, then we risk suppressing those emotions and can restrict the free flow of the life force, creating a chemical imbalance that may eventually show itself as physical pain.

NEGATIVE EMOTIONS

If you doubt how destructive our thoughts and emotions can be, just recall how you felt the last time you were upset, angry or stressed. Do you remember how the negative thoughts or emotions made you feel physically uncomfortable as your muscles tensed and your blood pressure rose, draining you of vital energy and leaving you feeling despondent and dispirited?

When we feel content, our mental energy is 'centred' (as it is in the chakras, our spiritual centres) and when we are excited or exercising our creative imagination it expands. But when we indulge in negative thoughts or are feeling stressed, we restrict the flow of mental energy and this leaves us literally depressed and may even manifest as physical pain.

HOW MEDITATION HEALS

Meditation helps to heal us because it puts us in touch with our emotions, thoughts and physical sensations. It puts impatience and intolerance into perspective and creates a sense of detachment that helps us keep our emotions in check.

Spiritual healing might not appear to be a meditation, but it is a perfect example of meditation in action. To attempt to heal other people, or at least to alleviate their suffering, is to practise a meditation on compassion, and this is arguably the most direct path to Enlightenment.

In everyday life
we rarely pay full
attention to anything,
whereas in meditation
practice we commit
ourselves exclusively
to doing just that.

HELPING TO HEAL ANOTHER

If you are giving someone a treatment, ask them to remove their glasses if they are wearing any, but to remain fully clothed. Get them to sit in an open-backed chair or on a stool so that you can treat their back. If they prefer lying down, ask them to turn over when you need to do their back. If this is not possible you will have to visualize the healing force penetrating through the front of the body to permeate each and every cell until it is absorbed into the muscles of the neck, spine and back.

If you want to send absent healing to someone, simply visualize them sitting with their back to you and affirm that they will receive this healing energy wherever they are at that moment.

It is not necessary to touch the person you wish to treat. You can just work on the spiritual aura that surrounds their physical body, but even then, make initial contact by placing your hands on their shoulders until you feel you are in tune with them. They do not need to enter a meditative state, although of course they can if they wish to.

SIMPLE HEALING

Before beginning this exercise make sure you are grounded by working through the exercise described on pages 53-54.

1. When you feel 'centred' and suitably relaxed, place your hands on the shoulders of the person you wish to heal. Acknowledge that you are not the source of this force and keep this in your mind as you direct the energy to the various parts of the body.

2. When you feel that the energy is flowing and that your auras have merged, start at the crown of the head and work your way down the person's body, giving equal emphasis to every area and smoothing the aura as you go. Become acutely aware of any areas that might feel cold or where you may sense resistance. The person you are treating may have indicated what their symptoms are, but it will not necessarily be where the source of the problem lies. The meditative state you are in will sensitize you to the still, small voice of your inner guide who may move your hands to where the healing needs to be concentrated.

3. It is important to see the healing process taking place and to picture the person you are treating in perfect health while you are giving them a treatment. But whatever insights you gain, do not be tempted to make a diagnosis of their problems if you are not a fully qualified medical practitioner. Also do not make any claims to healing powers or make promises of any kind whatsoever. If you are successful, they will feel better and you will benefit by having opened yourself to the 'Universal Force'.

4. End the session with a blessing or affirmation and let the person sit for a few moments to 'ground' them in case they feel slightly unbalanced by the surge of energy that they have received.

If you are healing in person, or are in contact with someone who is elderly or ill, it is always a good idea to enter a meditative state even while you are talking to them. Ground yourself and always channel the energy so that you both can benefit. If you do not feel able to give healing for any reason, then at least protect yourself by visualizing a metal plate in front of your solar plexus or a ball of light encasing you from head to toe.

SPREADING THE LIGHT

If you are concerned about negative influences that are around you in your own neighbourhood and beyond, you can use a variation on this meditation.

When you meditate, visualize yourself generating white light from a warm spot in your solar plexus. Visualize that light blending with light that you draw up from the ground through your feet and light that you draw down from the air.

1. When you feel 'centred' and energized, visualize that light spreading out from you like a beacon throughout your immediate environment. Visualize its blinding intensity spreading through the streets of your town and beyond through the county. See it being absorbed into the ground and being soaked up by a thirsty earth.

2. While you are channelling this energy through yourself say a quiet prayer or affirmation that serves to express your unconditional love for the whole of the planet and your fellow human beings to make you an even more open and efficient channel for the divine healing energy. When you are ready gradually return to waking consciousness.

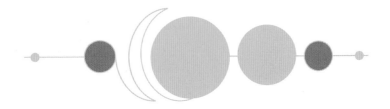

THE HEALING LIGHT

We have all been conditioned to believe that illness is inevitable and that it is only by maintaining a degree of physical fitness or taking prescribed drugs that we can fight infection or restore a breakdown in our biological functions. However, the basic principle of holistic health states that all physical symptoms are a manifestation of dis-ease in the emotional, mental or spiritual bodies and that we can eliminate illness, or at least limit its physical effects, by instilling our subconscious with positive life-affirming images.

WHY WE GET ILL

More commonly, illness can represent an inner conflict or a suppressed emotion that eats away at the healthy cells in the body like a parasite.

In every case meditation used on its own, or as a supplement to orthodox or complementary medicine, can help to relieve pain and reduce the anxiety that often aggravates the illness. It can also be used to reprogramme the subconscious mind so that negative thought patterns are effectively erased, making a recurrence of illness unlikely.

RAISING YOUR ENERGY

If you are ill, or just feeling run down and in need of revitalizing, the following exercise will help by stimulating every cell in your body and dissolving blockages that prevent the circulation of vital energy. It is also an ideal exercise to start the day, so try to fit it into your routine. Alternatively, if you need a boost at any time of the day, take five minutes out to raise your energy the natural way by following these simple steps, rather than drinking that extra cup of coffee or having a snack.

1. Get into your chosen position. Close your eyes and begin to focus on your breathing (see pages 37–38). Take a few deep breaths, then inhale deeply, hold it for a few moments, and then let the breath out as slowly and evenly as you can. Make a soft 'F' sound to push out the very last breath from the lungs so that you can start afresh.

2. Keeping a steady rhythm of breathing, begin to visualize a pool of soft white light at your feet. See it condensing like a luminous mist as you begin to draw it up around your ankles. Sense its gentle but penetrating warmth on the soles of your feet, then caressing your toes and your ankles as you begin to absorb the light into your body.

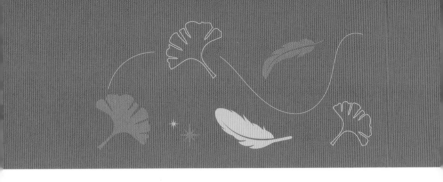

3. See and feel the warm, vibrant light soaking into your lower legs as if your skin were a sponge. The light is cleansing every cell and every blood vessel, stimulating the circulation of the subtle energies and the vital fluids as it rises from your knees up through your thighs to your hips and lower back.

4. Become aware of the light seeping into your lower and upper back, dissolving any blockages there and allowing the free flow of vital energy to every cell in your system. Feel the light flowing into any remaining areas of tension and kneading the knots in your muscles until they are totally relaxed.

5. The light now flows down through your arms to your hands and fingertips. See the light spreading out along the network of nerves and veins to your neck and into your head, relaxing your facial muscles and caressing your temples until you feel clear-headed and calm.

6. When you feel ready, open your eyes, but take a few moments to enjoy the peace before returning to your work or other tasks. Envisage this light surrounding you all day.

CELESTIAL BODIES

If you meditate on the sun or moon, or if they appear spontaneously in a meditation, it can symbolize the blossoming of male or female qualities.

THE SYMBOL OF THE MOON

The moon is a universal symbol of the passive, feminine principle. Therefore meditating on the moon, or having it spontaneously appear during a meditation, can indicate the awakening of the feminine qualities of intuition, sensitivity, creativity and compassion in both men and women.

The full moon is said to represent completion or wholeness and is widely associated with love, marriage and the family. It can therefore be quite useful to meditate on this image if you have to make a difficult decision regarding a relationship, although you must always balance what you think is guidance from the subconscious with input from the conscious mind's stock of common sense.

The ego is a great deceiver. We invariably believe what we want to believe and hear what we want to hear. Often what is 'right' for us is contrary to what we desire. Always test whatever comes through during meditation by asking yourself if it appeared spontaneously and if you were able to manipulate the images. If the imagery had a life of its own and you feel comfortable with it, then consider it as useful advice until you develop your intuition to the extent that you 'know' something has come from your 'Higher Self' and can act on it with confidence.

A FEMALE FIGUREHEAD

Many psychologists would interpret the moon as being symbolic of a significant female figure, usually a sister, mother or partner whose influence is becoming stronger or a person to whom you feel increasingly indifferent, for on an emotional level the moon is traditionally thought of as being 'cold'. If there is difficulty with a female figure in a relationship you can help to resolve it by visualizing yourself in the company of this person, preferably sitting by a lake in the moonlight and imagining a conversation with them. The setting will help to calm you and the image of the moon should stimulate the subconscious to bring all your thoughts on this subject to the surface.

You may have to 'write' the dialogue initially, but after a while the 'conversation' should become a natural, flowing exchange between your conscious and subconscious mind that may awaken feelings that you have not consciously expressed and might even offer solutions which you have not yet considered. Prepare to be surprised by yourself.

THE SYMBOL OF THE SUN

The sun is a universal symbol of the masculine principle, of the 'Universal Life Force', of healing, vitality and wisdom. Meditating on the sun, or having it appear spontaneously during a meditation, can indicate the awakening of ambition and determination.

If the rising sun appears during meditation, it can signify rebirth, the strengthening of the connection with your 'Higher Self', whereas the setting sun indicates the end of a specific phase in life and a need to rest before the next phase begins.

THE SUN FOR STRENGTH

If you are depleted of energy after a period of illness, feeling lethargic for any reason or have lost your enthusiasm for life you may find that meditating on the symbol of the sun will restore your strength. Simply imagine yourself in a beautiful garden or on a beach with the sun overhead and absorb its healing rays as if you were spiritually sunbathing. If you have an infection, whether it is a cold or something more serious, it can be beneficial to visualize the rays penetrating your skin and the sunlight being absorbed into your infected cells. See these as having a dark core and watch as the light burns them away until there is nothing left in your body but healthy cells.

Imagine yourself in a beautiful garden or on a beach with the sun overhead and absorb its healing rays.

VISUALIZATION

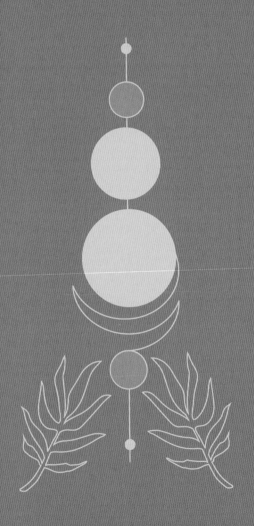

Visualization exercises, or meditations using the active imagination, are not only beneficial for relaxation. Before we can become what we want to be, or acquire what we want, we need to impress our desires on the unconscious and on the ether so that opportunities will arise and we will be ready to make full use of them. The following exercises will enable you to identify your short- and long-term goals, boost your self-confidence and improve your self-image through the use of creative visualization techniques. There are also exercises designed to help you to begin exploring your inner state, to create an inner sanctuary and to seek guidance from your 'Higher Self'.

WHAT IS VISUALIZATION?

One of the most common difficulties that I have encountered when teaching meditation is the number of people who are convinced that they cannot visualize. These days we tend to use our intellect far more than our imagination, or intuition, and so we frequently find it easier to focus on a physical object or an abstract idea rather than an image created in our mind's eye. We think through our problems and rationalize everything until there is little mystery left in life and everything that remains unexplained is dismissed because it cannot be proven to exist.

However, at the heart of the esoteric traditions of both East and West is the belief that our physical world is an illusion behind which exists a 'Greater Reality'. It is difficult for most of us to accept this because everything in the physical world seems real to our five senses. We can touch, taste, smell, see or hear everything with the exception of fresh air and electricity which we know to be real from observing their physical effects. And yet science has only recently proven the existence of dark matter, particles that are so tiny that they pass through the Earth in an unceasing stream without us being aware of them.

Once we accept that there is no solid matter as we perceive it, that matter is really only energy moving at such a low frequency that it is given the illusion of form, then we are nearer to accepting that there are worlds within worlds existing at subatomic levels where our spirit is thought to have its reality. The key to this inner dimension is the imagination, for the imagination is the medium through which we focus our mental energy to create our own happiness or hardship in this

world, and our own heaven and hell in the next.

THE SCOPE OF VISUALIZATIONS

Affirmations, mindfulness and the other techniques that I have introduced you to all have their benefits, but visualizations are almost limitless in how they can be used. They can attract whatever you want in life by clearing negative conditioning that may have 'programmed' you to believe that you were inferior to others, that you must suffer in life, or that it is 'wrong' to be wealthy, for example. They can help your mind to heal your body by channelling universal energy to revitalize the affected cells and strengthen the immune system. Visualizations can also bring about communication with your 'Higher Self' for the purposes of guidance and personal growth.

HOW VISUALIZATIONS WORK

Visualizations work by using the symbols and imagery that constitute the language of the subconscious. To achieve a particular end you need to programme your subconscious by placing the appropriate image in your mind's eye. In these meditations you can then either control the scene or let the events unfold under their own momentum. Another technique is to allow to arise spontaneously from the subconscious images that can be analysed after you have returned to waking consciousness. Whatever form of meditation you practise it is important that you develop your imagination, and that you persist in this even if you find it difficult at first.

HOW TO VISUALIZE

This is a basic exercise to get you used to the visualization process.

1. Get into your chosen position. Close your eyes, breathe naturally and relax. Visualize your immediate surroundings, picturing every object in the room as vividly and in as much detail as you can.

2. Next, imagine leaving the room and passing slowly through the building until you reach the front door noting everything as you go. Leave the building and walk around the neighbourhood. A walk around the block and back is sufficient for the initial excursions.

3. Visualize your tour with full sensory perception. Can you feel the breeze on your face, the contours of the ground, the warmth or chill in the air? Listen to the sounds that you normally take for granted. When you are ready, return the way you came. Do not rush but retrace your steps in detail. Then sense the weight of your body on the chair or bed and slowly open your eyes.

THE NIGHTLY REVIEW

This exercise is excellent for sharpening visual recall and disciplining your mind to follow a linear story. It is also very useful if you have trouble falling asleep.

1. Every night before you go to sleep, close your eyes and recall the events of the day in reverse order, from that evening back to when you awoke that morning. If you fall asleep before you reach the end, do not worry, you probably need the rest.

2. Do not simply catalogue the events but re-run them and visualize them in as much detail as you can. Sharpen your psychic senses and try to get a real sense of the atmosphere, sounds, smells, physical sensations and tastes.

3. Try to cultivate a sense of detachment so that you do not take everything personally, but rather accept these things as having been experienced by the body that you are inhabiting. Then let go and visualize a stream of images like a roll of movie film disappearing into the night sky to become part of the Akashic Records, or 'world memory'. This day is now part of the past. You cannot relive it. Let it go and affirm that tomorrow you will live every moment for the present.

> The imagination is the medium through which we focus our mental energy to create our own happiness.

ACHIEVING SUCCESS WITH VISUALIZATION

For creative visualization to be effective you need to have a strong desire to achieve something and not simply be curious, for example, to know what it might be like to drive a fast car or have your boss's job. The ideal subject for a visualization is something for which you have a strong and consistent yearning, that you feel is rightfully yours and that you strongly believe you are capable of achieving, given the opportunity. Creative visualization will create that opportunity, but it will always be up to you whether you take it and make of it what you originally imagined.

You also need to be willing to accept what you attract. Some people are actually frightened of success because they doubt that they can cope with it, that they are incapable of commitment, or that they are not deserving of its

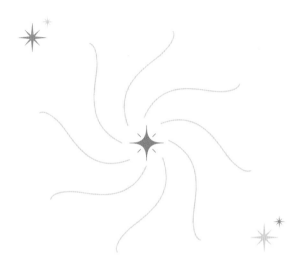

rewards. So they are constantly in pursuit of something that they subconsciously hope they will never obtain and to ensure that they never obtain it they frequently undermine their own efforts by deliberately missing important appointments or provoking those that they wish to impress.

So, if you want visualizations to work for you, be honest with yourself. In meditation ask your guide if you really want this particular thing and envisage the consequences if your wish is granted.

Another essential prerequisite states that your aim should be clearly defined. Asking for a 'better job' and limiting your visualization to a scene in which you see yourself lounging behind a big desk, or buying an expensive

> **For creative visualization to be effective you need to have a strong desire to achieve something and not simply be curious.**

new car, will not send the right message to the subconscious. You might win a new car with the road tax bills and running expenses that go with it, or you might find yourself assigned to a new office with nothing to do all day, but you will not be offered more satisfying and challenging work unless you send direct signals to the subconscious.

However, it is also not a good idea to go into too much detail as you may be blocking what is right for you by insisting that it comes in a particular package. What we think we want in our normal waking state is what the ego wants to satisfy its immediate and transient desires. But the basis of our personality, the 'Higher Self', knows what it needs to experience in this lifetime for its long-term development and it will invariably be greater than anything that you could have imagined yourself.

It is particularly important that you do not put faces to a partner, child or friend that you might be hoping to attract into your life. Again, your 'Higher Self' knows who is right for you to meet in order that you can both learn the lessons that you need to learn in this life. It will interfere with your own chosen life pattern if you try to impose a personality upon the subconscious. Instead be open and willing to accept whoever the Universe (the divine source) sends. In the case of a prospective partner or friend you will still have the free will to commit yourself to that relationship or not, as you see fit.

To ensure that you are open to whatever is right for you, use this affirmation, or words of your own choice, while you are picturing a particular scene and just before returning to waking consciousness. 'Whatever is right for me is now manifesting in the Universe for the highest good of all concerned.'

BUILDING THE FUTURE

The following exercise is deceptively simple, but surprisingly effective. Use it every time that you feel anxious about the future or begin to doubt your abilities. You can also use it periodically to top up your self-confidence. If you do so, you will find that your confidence and self-esteem will steadily increase until your anxieties about the present or future go away.

Get into your chosen position (see pages 31–33). Close your eyes, breathe naturally (see pages 37–38) and sink into a deep state of relaxation.

1. Think back to your earliest memories of childhood, to a time when you achieved something that surprised you and made you feel happy. Perhaps it was a physical feat, such as jumping over something that had seemed impossible for you at that age, or finding your first friend, or being brave when you went to nursery school for the first time. Our memories of childhood are usually vague, but everyone can remember something significant from their early years if they think hard enough. Trust that something will come to the surface and it will, for everything that you have done and everything that you have said has been imprinted on

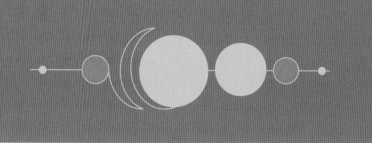

the subconscious. The important thing is that it should be something that pleased you, not necessarily something for which you received approval.

2. When you have a scene in mind, scan it for details. Take in as much of the sounds, smells and tastes as you possibly can. If you feel yourself becoming emotional, let the feelings flow because it is obviously something that needs to be expressed and cleared.

3. Now scan forward slowly to another incident in your childhood when you made another step forward in understanding or proved your physical ability. Perhaps it was learning to swim or ride a bike. Can you remember if you were anxious about doing this, or maybe you doubted your ability. Can you also recall the feeling when you succeeded?

4. Continue like this through school, further education, your first job, relationships, setting up home and other incidents to the present moment. Let the images come to you naturally and then, when you are ready, come back to waking consciousness.

LIMITLESS ASPIRATIONS

There are no limitations to what you can attract, only your willingness to accept what is possible. If your reward is something simple that you can enjoy now, then do it. You will feel better for having treated yourself and you will attract more good fortune into your life by acting in anticipation of the promise of more to come. But if you are frightened of acting, justifying your reluctance to take risks by imagining that you are being prudent and sensible, then you are, in effect, reinforcing your fear on your subconscious. If you deny yourself something that you really want and can afford, then you are telling yourself that when that money is gone there will be no more. Of course if you sincerely believe that, then there will not be any more.

IMPROVING YOUR SELF-IMAGE

An unfortunate habit that many of us indulge in from time to time involves comparing ourselves to others. It is almost certain to result in disappointment for the simple reason that everybody is unique, possessing qualities and failings in unequal measure, according to what they have experienced in previous lives and what they need to learn in this incarnation. The Buddhist philosophy states that instead of considering ourselves as competing individuals we should be refining our true nature so that it can reflect this unique side of us without distortion.

But to do this we first need to free ourselves of the false image that we have of ourselves which goes no deeper than the physical shell, and which is coloured by the comments and conditioning on which our ego depends for its reality.

SELF-PORTRAIT

Get into your chosen position (see pages 31–33). Close your eyes and relax into a regular rhythm of breathing (see pages 37–38). Visualize yourself in an art gallery standing before a full-length portrait of yourself as you were when you were really happy.

1. Take a long look at yourself and consider what you see in those eyes, in the facial features and in the way that you hold yourself. What type of character has the artist captured?

2. Now you hear approaching footsteps. A small crowd of friends, and family members has come to admire your portrait and tell you why they love or respect you. There is no need to be self-conscious or to display false modesty. In this dimension everyone speaks the truth. This occasion is not the place for criticism, but for appreciation and deserving praise. This is not an empty gesture, but a demonstration of genuine affection.

3. See each person in turn as they approach the portrait and listen as they declare your qualities to the group. You may be surprised by what they reveal. Others often admire us for qualities that we may take for granted.

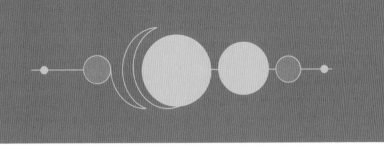

4. When everyone has spoken their piece take another long look at the portrait. Has it changed? If so, in what way? In the light of what has been said by your friends and family do you think that you have been too self-critical in the past? Have you been driving yourself too hard rather than treating yourself as you would your best friend?

5. Now consider, if all these people love you for the reasons that they have stated, then how can you not love yourself?

6. Look at the portrait for the last time and in your own words affirm that you are a loving, intelligent, creative person. Find other thoughts that come to mind. Use whatever attributes you can recall other people saying. Then, when you have finished, gradually return to waking consciousness.

APPRECIATING YOUR LIFE

As an adjunct to this exercise and the meditation on the previous page it is a good idea to put yourself into a meditative mood a couple of times a week and make a mental inventory of all those things in your life that give you pleasure. These can range from your state of health or your sense of humour to the companionship of your friends or even possessions which you appreciate.

Some people feel guilty about having a wealth of possessions and material comforts, but it is important to accept what the universe has provided and also to accept that we live in an abundant world where there is plenty of everything for everybody. Putting any conditions or limitations on your happiness and success does not help any of those who have less. It simply restricts your

powers to manifest what you want and have the right to have in your own life.

Whether you consider these 'blessings' to be gifts from God, symbols of good fortune or the reward for hard work is not important. What you are doing by recalling these things to mind is reinforcing your image of yourself as a healthy, happy and attractive personality with the ability to attract what you want into your life. Enjoy it.

SETTING YOURSELF GOALS

Creative visualization can also be used to clarify your aims in life and find out what is really important to you at a particular point in your life.

The American personal growth guru Shakti Gawain, author of *Creative Visualization* and *Living in the Light*, gives several examples of how to do so, including the making of a 'wish list' and visualizing an ideal scene.

In the former, all you have to do is draw up a list of things that you want to achieve under the appropriate headings.
These include:
Work/Career, Money, Lifestyle/Possessions, Relationships, Creative Self-Expression, Leisure/Travel and Personal Growth/Education.

If, for example, you want a more satisfying job, write a brief and unambiguous sentence under the heading 'Work/Career' along the lines of 'I want a more satisfying and better-paid job which will be right for me in every respect, which will not require me to commute or move away from here and which will still leave me time for my family'. If you are not specific about what you want, you may be offered more satisfying work, but it might require you to move to the other end of the country and to work longer hours. Of course you always have the free will to refuse the offer, but if you are desperate for work you may feel obliged to take it.

ACHIEVING YOUR GOALS

Exercises of this nature may not appear to be meditations in the traditional sense, but they require a similar degree of heightened concentration and awareness that will bring secret hopes to the surface. We all think we know what we want to ensure our happiness, but until we focus our minds in this way, we tend to drift through life with only a vague idea of what we are aiming for and put our trust in fate. Without a clear idea of what we want in our lives we will not be able to create it, because there will be no goal towards which we can channel our mental energy.

CREATING YOUR IDEAL WORLD

Write down the first of the seven categories listed on this page at the top of a large blank piece of paper, then get into your chosen position (see pages 31-33). Close your eyes, breathe naturally (see pages 37-38) and meditate on that theme, allowing your ideal scene to form in its own time. It is the quality of your life that you are looking to improve, so in the first meditation on the theme of Work/Career it is important to see yourself being relaxed and pleased with your work, rather than simply being successful. Do not limit yourself; be generous. In freeing your imagination in this way you could be surprised to discover aims and ideas of which you were previously unaware.

When you have finished your meditation, gradually return to waking consciousness and write down everything that you can remember. Then do the same with the second category until you have a paragraph or two for each of the seven scenes.

SETTING TIME LIMITS

Now read through what you have written down and choose ten specific goals that you can identify. Then select those which you can imagine achieving over the course of the next five years and write these down in a new list under the heading 'Five-year Goals'.

Do the same again for those which seem to be realistic aims for the coming year, and finally list those which you feel comfortable aiming to fulfil within the next six months.

Clarifying your short-term goals in this way will help you to identify the stages that you need in order to achieve your long-term ambitions, so that they do not remain mere fantasies. But do not aim too high or you will soon lose heart if you fail to fulfil the

short-term steps. Above all, keep them simple and choose goals that will make you feel great when you succeed, rather than choosing things that you feel you ought to achieve to fulfil someone else's expectations.

THE INNER SANCTUARY

Every person exists on several levels of reality simultaneously – the physical, emotional, mental and spiritual realms. When we meditate, we raise our awareness of these levels as we rise in consciousness from the purely physical to examine our feelings and then our thoughts,

Be mindful of every
movement as you walk
rather than losing yourself
in your own thoughts.

and, ultimately, expand our consciousness beyond the physical senses.

It is therefore important that, after creating 'sacred space' in which to work on the physical plane, that we do the same on the inner planes where the process of transformation can continue. To do this we can use visualization to create a garden where we can seek sanctuary whenever we need to withdraw momentarily from the world. Many people think that this is merely exercising the imagination, but just as our soul exists in a dimension that we are rarely conscious of, so the garden will have its reality in the inner realm as a 'thought form', brought into existence by you with each successive meditation.

THE SYMBOLIC GARDEN

The garden is an archetypal image common to many spiritual traditions that might otherwise appear incompatible on the surface. The *Kabbalah*, for example, envisages existence as a series of four interpenetrating worlds of increasing refinement in which the psychological realm is symbolized as a pastoral paradise. This was mythologized in the Old Testament as the Garden of Eden and is the source of the Christian concept of Heaven. It is no coincidence that the *Koran* (the sacred book of Islam) also describes the realms beyond our own as four Gardens of Paradise, for the Islamic mystics shared the same image of the structure of existence.

We should also not be surprised that the same imagery recurs in innumerable modern accounts of near-death experiences described by ordinary individuals with no particular religious conviction, for the garden is a universal symbol of the sacred space in which the soul has its reality.

Every person exists on several levels of reality simultaneously – the physical, emotional, mental and spiritual realms.

THE WALLED GARDEN

Make yourself comfortable and get into your chosen position (see pages 31–33). Close your eyes and breathe naturally, relaxing into a regular rhythm (see pages 37–38). When you feel ready, visualize yourself standing before the entrance to a walled garden; perhaps it is a door covered with vines or an iron gate through which you can glimpse the garden beyond.

1. Enter the garden and look around you. What are your first impressions? Is it a rambling cottage garden or laid out in a neat, formal design? Is it well kept or neglected? Are there weeds and thistles among the flowers? Are there fruit trees or vegetables?

2. Can you smell the scent of the flowers? Can you hear the droning of bees or the sweet singing of birds? Can you feel the breeze on your face? Can you get a sense of what the flowers feel like to the touch? Pick up a handful of soil. Is it dry and lifeless or friable and rich in nutrients? Is it sticky and clay-like?

3. Look at the sky. Is it overcast or clear? What season is it? Look at the wall that encloses the garden. Is it low,

head-height or unusually high and imposing? Are there any special features such as a sundial, a raised bed of herbs or a pond?

4. Is there somewhere you can sit and contemplate your surroundings or think over a problem? If not, now is the time to create one. You might also wish to get started on tidying up the flower beds, sweeping the paths, cutting the grass, pruning dead flower heads and so on. But this is not work. It requires no effort, only the will to make your vision a reality and create a sanctuary in a world beyond your imagination.

5. It is here that you can invite your guide to join you whenever you need help or advice and you can be confident that you will receive it. But now it is time to return slowly to waking consciousness, bringing the peace of this place with you back into the 'real world'. Record all your impressions in your journal.

THE PATH TO INNER PEACE

This section offers advanced techniques to bring variety and greater depth to your practice, and for safely probing deeper into the psyche. After a look at the value of mantras and music and an outline describing how to incorporate them into your routine there is a description of the relationship between the chakras of the Hindu tradition and the sephiroth of the Kabbalistic system.

Exercises include the 'Middle Pillar' visualization for clearing and centring the chakras, a 'Pathworking' for exploring a specific area of the psyche and a method for exploring past lives.

MANTRAS

From the earliest times monks and mystics have used mantras and chants to induce a trance-like state. Many cultures and traditions, including the ancient Egyptians, adhered to the belief that existence itself was created by sound (a concept adopted by the early Christians who conceived of 'The Word' as the manifest expression of God). Even today certain sounds are held to be sacred in the Hindu and Vedic traditions, while Jewish law forbids the name of God to be spoken in the belief that it can facilitate the act of creation (a belief which gave rise to the 'words of power' venerated by the medieval magicians).

It was not until the 1960s that the connection between sound and physical form was proven scientifically by Hans Jenny. He discovered that specific sounds produced consistent, symmetrical patterns that bore a striking resemblance to certain Eastern mandalas, which are symbolic images of universal harmony used in meditation. The Swiss psychologist, Carl Jung, had earlier concluded that the power of mandalas is due to the fact that they represent stages in the integration of the psyche.

STILLING THE MIND

It is thought that every living organism emits its own unique vibration which is translated in the strength and colours of the aura. For that reason those who practise Transcendental Meditation (TM) (see pages 17–19) are given a personal mantra which is an expression of their unique vibration. However, TM is an exception and has been criticized for creating an atmosphere of exclusivity which is contrary to the principles of spiritual practice. The majority of mantras are simply words or phrases designed to still the mind and can be freely used by anyone. One of the most commonly used chants is the Buddhist benediction 'Aum mani padme hum', which roughly translates as 'Hail to the jewel in the lotus', an acknowledgement of

the Buddha nature that is present in us all.

The chanting of mantras remains a central practice in Buddhist meditation where the sounds themselves have a mystical significance. For example, 'O' is considered to be the sound of unity and perfection, 'U' represents the descent of spirit into matter, 'A' expresses intellect

Contact with the
unconscious is made
through the imagination,
but the images are not a
product of the imagination.

and communication, 'H' is the sound of the breath and therefore of life, while 'M' is the sound between the unity of spirit and the duality of matter.

In the Eastern tradition the three primary sounds on which most mantras are based are seen as expressions of the mind, body and spoken word. 'OM' is the transcendent Universal Unity, 'AH' is the fully realized human being and 'HUM' is the individual.

PRACTISING MANTRAS IN THE WEST

Many Western meditation groups introduce mantras so that students can experience the effects for themselves. However, few Westerners adopt the practice as part of their regular routine because they feel self-conscious or are uncomfortable with repeating a phrase in a language that they do not understand.

But every tradition has suitable phrases that can be freely adopted, and for those who do not subscribe to a particular faith or philosophy, the chanting of one's own name is said to be equally effective. Alternatively, if you have a particular goal in mind, such as stopping smoking or increasing your self-confidence, you can use a suitable affirmation which the cyclic chanting will help to imprint in your subconscious. Otherwise a single word such as 'Relax' is sufficient to induce a feeling of calm prior to an important meeting or at the end of a busy day.

USING MANTRAS

Get into your chosen position (see pages 31–33). Take as
deep a breath as you can, then let the air out as slowly and
evenly as you can while chanting your chosen phrase. The
sound should be said as loud and as clearly as possible
so that its vibration creates sympathetic resonance in
your chest.

1. Endeavour to create a continuous loop so that the end
of the phrase melts into the beginning of the next. Keep
the intonation and rhythm even, synchronized with your
breathing or heartbeat so that the monotony of the sound
becomes hypnotic.

2. If you wish you can gradually reduce the volume of your
voice until the chant is created in your mind. Then allow it
to dissipate and immerse yourself in the ensuing stillness.

3. Try not to think about the meaning of the mantra but
rather let it become a meaningless sound in which you are
absorbed. Let the last intonation fade away naturally and
gradually return to waking consciousness.

MUSIC FOR MEDITATION

Music has proven to be a wonderful aid to meditation, providing a focus to help still the mind and attune it to specific states of consciousness. In the East the use of bells, drums, other instruments and single sustained notes has long been an integral part of the meditation ritual, whereas in the West it has been an important feature of ceremonial worship, as an aid to contemplation rather than meditation.

It was not until the 18th century that the potential therapeutic value of music was taken seriously in the West. Count Keyserling, a Russian envoy, was suffering from insomnia and in desperation commissioned the German composer Johann Sebastian Bach to write a piece of light music to soothe his nerves. The next time he could not sleep the Count summoned a harpsichord player, Johann Goldberg, and asked him to play the specially written piece of music. Within minutes the Count fell soundly asleep.

This piece of music and subsequent compositions by Bach, which were collectively known as the *Goldberg Variations*, were the subject of scientific study in the 1970s by Dr Georgi Lozanov. The Bulgarian scientist discovered that the opening and closing theme of each variation induced a meditative state by slowing down the body's biological functions. The same effect was found to be an intrinsic characteristic of other slow movements by composers of the Baroque period, namely Handel, Vivaldi, Telemann and Corelli.

Now, recent studies suggest that instrumental music, particularly those movements with a constant tempo of 60 beats per minute, can be an invaluable aid in reprogramming the subconscious mind with positive suggestions to aid healing and achieve personal goals. It appears that the steady, regular tempo and predictable harmonic progression serves to induce alpha states, which is a sense of relaxed alertness in which the brain assimilates and retains information more readily.

AUTOGENIC TRAINING

This is one particularly well-known form of complementary therapy in which visualizations are enhanced by music to achieve specific purposes, such as increasing self-confidence or inducing restful sleep. The technique was developed in the 1920s by the German psychiatrist Johannes H. Schulz who discovered that by focusing on the weight and

When consciousness is raised to the point of the eighth chakra a person will attain union with their 'Higher Self'.

> **We all have the tendency to burden ourselves with emotional baggage from our past.**

warmth of the body his patients relaxed automatically. In this state he also found that they were more receptive to suggestions and able to overcome any resistance that had been created by long-term conditioning.

CHOOSING THE RIGHT MUSIC

As a general rule any music which has a constant pulse of 60 beats per minute will induce the relaxation response, but each piece will trigger a specific emotion or quality because its dominant tone creates a vibrational frequency that corresponds to one of the major chakras. It is no coincidence that there are eight notes in the octave (seven different notes with the eighth being a repetition of the root) and seven major chakras. When consciousness is raised to the point of the eighth chakra, a person will attain union with their

'Higher Self' and a new octave of awareness unfolds.

CLEARING NEGATIVE EMOTIONS

In the Buddhist tradition there is an allegorical tale of two monks who were returning to their monastery from a pilgrimage when they came upon an old woman sitting by a fast-flowing stream. The old woman asked the monks if they could help her to cross and one of them immediately offered to carry her on his back. When he had done so he returned to find that his companion had not waited for him and was already some distance away. When he eventually caught up with him, he found him to be silent and rather sullen so asked him what was causing him such pain. 'Monks are forbidden from physical contact with women', said the sullen monk. 'Indeed,' replied the first, 'but I put her down safely on the far

bank an hour ago and you are still carrying her.'

We all have the tendency to burden ourselves with emotional baggage from our past, even when we know that it is impeding our future progress. The following exercise will help you to clear deeply rooted thought patterns created by painful past memories, persistent regrets or nagging resentments.

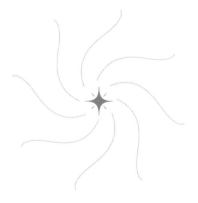

CLEARING OUT THE PAST

Get into your chosen position (see pages 31–33). Close your eyes and breathe naturally, getting into a regular rhythm (see pages 37–38). When you are sufficiently relaxed visualize a remote mountain track leading to a temple a few hundred metres from where you are now standing.

1. You begin to walk up the track toward the temple and as you approach you can hear the sound of muted voices chanting a mantra that stirs emotions deep within you. The primal sound invites you to go within.

2. You pause at the entrance and remove your shoes. The door is ajar and an elderly monk sitting just within the entrance beckons you inside. In the half-light you see a line of Buddhist monks sitting cross-legged on either side from the door to the altar.

3. Now walk towards the altar at the far end; it is decorated in a gold-coloured cloth engraved with images of Buddha. Here bowls of water and fruit adorn the altar. Perhaps you have brought an offering that you can add. If so, what is it?

4. Before you is a low stool on which rest some sheets of paper and a pen. Sitting cross-legged before the altar you

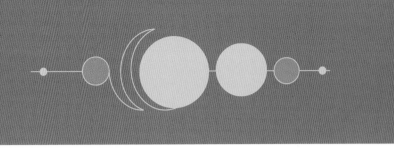

begin to write whatever regrets you may be clinging to; whatever memories bring you pain and the resentments that you may be harbouring from the past. Now is the time to soften your heart centre, express what is deeply felt but unspoken and offer all these regrets to the purifying flame that is the light of the Buddha of compassion.

5. When you have finished, fold the paper into a taper and place it in the burning bowl sitting at the feet of the Buddha. Watch as the paper shrivels into ash and affirm in words of your own choosing that you are now relieved of all those things that have burdened you for too long.

6. Forgive yourself and accept whatever happened to you as a learning experience.

7. Remain seated before the altar, contemplating the symbol of your own Buddha nature and the serenity within. Know that the only thing separating you from your divine nature is your attachment to the transient things of the physical world. Let go of what you cannot control and be centred in yourself. When you feel ready, return to waking consciousness, count down slowly from ten to one and then open your eyes.

THE POWER OF POSITIVE THINKING

The book concludes with a look at affirmations and the potential that they offer for clearing negative conditioning, personal transformation and for freeing ourselves from bad habits. A 'meditation menu' offers a directory of scenarios for clearing resentment, cutting emotional ties, dealing with disappointment, dispelling fear and worry, coping with grief and loss, seeking guidance from the 'Higher Self' and using colour therapy in the context of a visualization.

AFFIRMATIONS

No matter how self-aware, intelligent and unique we consider ourselves to be, it is a fact that we are all highly suggestible. Our choice of consumer goods is largely dictated by marketing people, our world view is influenced by the media and our moods can be manipulated by the comments and attitudes of other people – if we allow them. But we can free ourselves from negative influences, harmful mental habits and the effects of long-term conditioning through reprogramming our subconscious minds with positive suggestions, known as affirmations. These can be used as a mantra in meditation to create positive patterns and thoughts so that we can transform our perception of ourselves and of the outside world.

One of the best-known affirmations is the phrase 'Every day in every way I am becoming better and better,' which has become a cliché of the self-help school of psychotherapy. But the most effective phrases are those which you create for yourself in your own words for specific aims such as finding the right partner, becoming more patient or being open to new opportunities.

CREATING YOUR OWN AFFIRMATIONS

Here are some guidelines for choosing your own affirmations.

- They should be short, simple, unambiguous and phrased to emphasize the positive. 'I have a fulfilling and well-paid job with time for myself in the evenings and at weekends,' will create the right image in the subconscious, whereas 'I don't want to work long hours in a poorly paid job,' will only serve to reinforce your frustration.

- Always express affirmations in the present tense, as if what you want already exists. If you use the future tense, you are implying that it might be conditional. You need to impress upon the subconscious that you expect your wish to be fulfilled.

- If you feel some resistance and you have checked that there is no ambiguity in the phrase you are using, persist, because if it is a long-term problem or attitude that you are trying to overcome it is likely that the ego will oppose it, just as it will have done when you first started to establish the habit of meditation.

- Reinforce the affirmation with a visualization on the same theme but be careful that you do not sketch in too many details, otherwise you risk putting limitations on what is right for you.

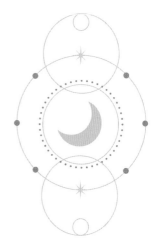

POSITIVE AFFIRMATIONS TO USE

'I am on my true path and every day leads me nearer to my true place.'

'I am complete and perfectly acceptable as I am.'

'I live in an abundant Universe and there is plenty for everybody.'

'I enjoy perfect health and peace of mind.'

'I am fulfilling the purpose of my life which is becoming clearer to me each day.'

'I am calm and "centred".'

'I exist in the present, I let go of the past.'

✳

No matter how self-aware, intelligent and unique we consider ourselves to be, it is a fact that we are all highly suggestible.

✳

MEDITATIONS FOR DIFFERENT MOODS

Being on the spiritual path does not mean that you are immune to the frustrations of modern life. In fact, the farther you go along the path the more your commitment is tested. Over the following six pages you will find meditations to help you to overcome specific problems.

I have sketched a possible scenario and provided suggestions for suitable affirmations to use in each case, but as you become more confident and experienced you may want to devise your own visualizations based on the principles which I have outlined in this book. Whichever path you take, may it lead you to your true place and to a life of fulfilment and peace.

CLEARING RESENTMENT

If ever you feel that you have been criticized unfairly and have been denied the opportunity to tell your side of the story, or if you have been taken for granted, use this method to clear any leftover resentment. If you do not clear it, your frustration will eat away at you bringing more harm to you than the person you hold responsible for your unhappiness.

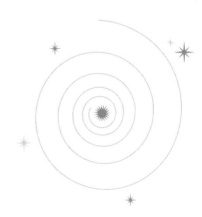

GETTING RID OF AN UPSET

Get into your chosen position (see pages 31–33). Close your eyes, breathe naturally and when you feel suitably relaxed imagine that you are sitting at a desk. In front of you are pen, paper, envelope, candle, matches and a bowl filled with water.

1. Look down at the blank paper in front of you and take up the pen. Now write a letter to the person who you believe has upset you, describing your feelings and explaining the situation as you understand it. It is necessary to express your feelings, as the primary purpose of this exercise is to face and free your emotions. Once you have released your anger you will hopefully see the situation from a less impassioned perspective and having done so you may now feel able to 'forgive and forget'.

2. When you have finished your letter imagine addressing the envelope (adding a description of the person if you do not know their name) and put the letter inside. Now ask your guide or 'Higher Self' to take it into the light. Visualize burning the envelope in the candle flame and when it has curled into ashes drop it into the bowl.

When you meditate there should be no effort to control and no attempt to be peaceful. Do not be overly solemn or feel that you are taking part in some special ritual.

DEALING WITH DISAPPOINTMENT

To feel disappointment is to discover how badly you wanted something. Whether the object of your ambition is worthy of your efforts and whether it is right for you is something that only honest reflection can reveal. If you are determined to achieve something you can ensure success by visualizing yourself planning the necessary steps to acquire it, and then seeing yourself having attained it as a present reality.

DISPELLING FEAR AND WORRY

Our imagination is the means through which we can create a new reality, but the thoughts and emotions which empower the process can be either negative or positive, so we have to be careful which variety we bring into being.

Although meditation should never be used to dwell on the negative if you are at the mercy of fearful thoughts, it can be useful to examine those fears in a visualization where you imagine the worst that could happen to you if your fears are realized. You might be surprised to discover that there is a limit to what can go wrong, and that it is not as bad as you had feared. Facing your fears head on in this way and naming them instead of allowing them to roam as vague, formless monsters in your nightmares should also be enough to strip them of their power over you.

COPING WITH GRIEF AND LOSS

Whether you have been recently bereaved or are grieving for the loss of something or someone that has meant a great deal to you, the following meditation should bring you comfort and peace of mind.

SEEKING EMOTIONAL PEACE

Get into your chosen position. Close your eyes, breathe naturally and when you feel suitably relaxed recall the happy times that you enjoyed. Think of those times as a gift that has enriched your life and is now an integral part of your character. Such experiences can never be taken from you. Understand that death is merely a transition from life to life, that our divine essence cannot die and that what we are grieving for is our loss and not their passing.

Consider the parable of the grief-stricken mother who begged Buddha to restore her dead child to life and was told to find a house that had never known death. In the pain of grief we forget that no one is immune from suffering and loss. We all die and we all leave someone behind to mourn our passing. If there was no one to grieve that would mean that our life had touched no one and that would indeed be a cause for sorrow.

RESOLVING DIFFICULTIES

It takes two to create difficulties in a relationship, so begin by altering your perception of the problem and 'centre' yourself so that you remain calm and objective in the midst of any upsets.

1. Get into your chosen position. Close your eyes, breathe naturally and when you feel suitably relaxed visualize the other person surrounded by white light which is the radiance of their spirit. Soften your heart centre by meditating on compassion. See the other person as a divine being whose human nature is as fallible as your own, but who is continually seeking perfection through experience.

2. Draw them towards you and embrace them while repeating the following affirmation: 'X and I are enjoying a good, positive relationship. Energy is flowing freely between us.' Then release them and watch as they fade into the distance.

3. If the relationship is right for you, the other person will sense a change in the atmosphere on a psychic level and should respond. Tension will be diffused and you will be able to talk matters through calmly.

SEEKING GUIDANCE

4. Choose or create an affirmation that relates to your present circumstances, or to the specific question that you wish to have answered and use it like a mantra to reveal the truth of the situation.

5. Relax into a meditative state and say your chosen sentence or ask your question once. Then listen for an answer. Let thoughts rise spontaneously but attach no importance to them until they cease to be random and meaningless. Repeat the affirmation or question a second time and listen again for a response. Repeat saying the two affirmations, once a day, on 11 consecutive days.

6. Long before the final session you should find yourself holding a conversation with your 'Higher Self' that will be spontaneous, natural and flowing and will contain insights that you could not possibly have obtained from your conscious mind.

7. You will know that this is a genuine communication rather than imagination because the words will flow faster than you can think of them.

PRACTISING
SELF-CONTROL

Whether you want to free yourself from a bad habit such as smoking, go on a diet or be more in control of your emotions, the following exercise should prove beneficial.

Get into your chosen position. Close your eyes, breathe naturally and when you feel suitably relaxed identify precisely what it is that you want to achieve. Consider if anything is preventing you from achieving your goal.

1. Visualize yourself overcoming those obstacles. If you simply visualize yourself achieving your aim, you will not be successful as your inner resistance will not have been addressed.

2. Gradually return to waking consciousness, note down any insights that you have received and act on them in anticipation of being successful. This will reinforce your resolve and make it easier to achieve your goal as you will not be struggling against any inner resistance.

COLOURS AND WELLBEING

Different colours can also help with emotional and intellectual issues.

Brown is the colour associated with the earth and can be used if you feel you need to be more practical and more in control of your passions.

Red is the colour of physical energy, so is an ideal choice for those who feel lethargic or who are recuperating from a long illness. Red can also dissolve arthritic crystals, heal genital disorders and stimulate the circulation.

Orange is the colour that relates to emotions so meditations using orange are often effective in dispelling anxiety, depression and stress-related disorders. Orange is also thought to improve digestion and heal disorders of the liver, pancreas and gall bladder.

COLOUR THERAPY

If you are experiencing any kind of problem worrying about it will only make matters worse. It focuses your mental energy inwards and can bring about fatigue and depression. Meditation expands the mind, alleviating the pressure and stimulating the release of endorphins – the body's natural painkillers.

Take time out to scan your
body for tension and give
your mind a rest, as it is
in stillness that inspiration
and insight will come.

Yellow represents the intellect and so is the colour to visualize if you need to make a difficult decision and you do not want to be confused by emotional issues. It is also good as an aid to study. It helps you to absorb more information, retain facts more effectively and recall them more readily. So meditate on the colour yellow before an important exam and you should experience less stress and achieve higher marks! Yellow is also traditionally identified with the regenerative power of the sun and is effective for healing on all levels – physical, emotional, mental and spiritual.

Green is the colour of nature and of harmony between the physical and spiritual realms. As such it is an effective calming colour and is useful for alleviating nervous complaints.

Blue is the traditional healing colour for all purely physical ailments, but it also corresponds to the throat chakra which means that blue is the colour to visualize if you need to communicate more effectively or stimulate your creative energies.

Purple is the colour associated with intuition and inspiration, so if you are looking for new

ideas immerse yourself in purple and listen for that inner voice. This is also the colour to work with if you want to raise your level of psychic sensitivity or stimulate your imagination.

Violet is the colour you will need if you want to strengthen your resolve and help yourself through testing times.

White is the colour of purity and the spiritual essence of us all, so meditating on white light puts you in touch with your spiritual guide and your own potential.

RELATIONSHIPS – CUTTING TIES

The mind has often been likened to a restless baby monkey that does not take readily to training and, like the monkey, it is also a creature of habit. We tend to cling to thoughts that give us the illusion of security, even when it is obvious that the time has come to let go of the past or be pragmatic and flexible in the rules we live by and the standards we set ourselves.

Reliving a failed relationship in your mind, reminiscing or indulging in recriminations and regrets do not alter the past, nor do they affect the person we may want to change. The only things that these negative habits do successfully are drain our vital energies and postpone our future happiness.

Whether you are finding it difficult to free yourself from an emotionally draining relationship that has clearly run its course, or you are harbouring resentment from a past wrong (whether real or imagined), you owe it to yourself, and to the other party, to release the bonds that bind you together and instead channel your energies into creating your future. The following visualization will help you to achieve this.

Reliving a failed
relationship
in your mind,
reminiscing or
indulging in
recriminations
and regrets
do not alter
the past.

LETTING GO

Get into your chosen position (see pages 31–33). Close your eyes and establish a regular breathing pattern (see pages 37–38). When you feel suitably relaxed, begin to visualize a small sphere of white light in the darkness directly in front of you. Watch as the light grows in size and intensity.

1. You begin to see a figure in the distance who you recognize as the person to whom you still feel emotionally bound. Observe them with detachment as they approach, for this is their spirit, their essence or true nature, and it shares the same source as you do. Whatever differences or misunderstandings may exist between you as personalities, in spirit you are brothers/sisters.

2. As you observe the other person, understand that the essence of that personality wishes you well and that the problem that you perceive to exist between you originates with the ego, yours and theirs. Consider it to be a clash between the two individual wills which should instead be conforming to the 'Universal Will' that desires happiness and fulfilment for both of you; a happiness that you cannot even imagine at this moment because you are too self-, or ego centred.

3. Try to forgive that person of whatever wrong you feel has been done to you and in turn ask forgiveness from them for creating this disharmony between you. Do not be tempted to apportion blame.

4. Now begin to see the strands of glistening particles that have bound you in spirit to that person which you have created with your emotionally charged thoughts. To free yourself from the emotional attachment to this person, visualize them dematerializing or being severed at the source. If you want to, you can call upon any deity, spiritual figure or discarnate being such as an angel, your guide or 'Higher Self' to assist you. You can then ask this being or the 'Universal Life Force' to bless both of you and illuminate your true path so that you might both find your true place (and partner if applicable) in this life.

5. Affirm that you have no further demands on this person and that you wish them well. Then watch as they return to the light and see the light dissolve. When you feel ready, count down slowly from ten to one and open your eyes. Remember, as you return to waking consciousness, that the person who most often requires your forgiveness, of course, is yourself.

CONCLUSION

In the West we are still preoccupied with the need to explain the mechanics and mysteries of the mind, whereas in the East the aim is to transcend it. For that reason many Westerners are puzzled and perhaps even put off taking up meditation by talk of 'surrendering to the Higher Self', of 'emptying the mind' and of 'meditating on nothingness' in an effort to discover one's 'true nature'.

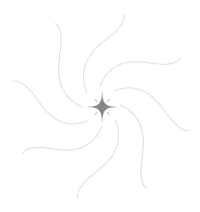

Such terms might strike some as abstract or irrational, but the meditative state of relaxed awareness is a state to which we all ought to aspire for the sake of our spiritual, mental, emotional and physical wellbeing. Throughout this book, we have explained that it is not necessary to subscribe to any particular belief system or philosophy to practise meditation.

However, to deny the spiritual tradition from which it evolved would be to limit its potential for personal transformation before the journey had even begun.